SUMMER MATH WORKBOOK

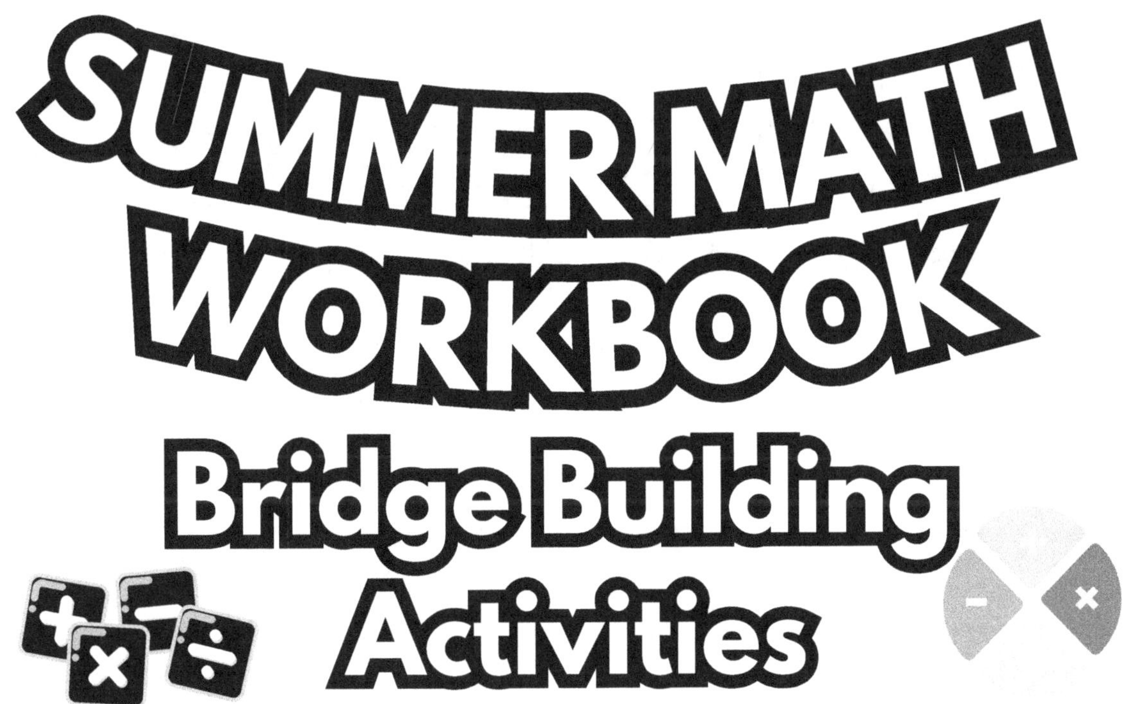

Grade
5 → 6
SUMMER MATH WORKBOOK
Bridge Building Activities
Multiplication and Division
Factors and Multiples
Fractions and Geometry

Grade
6 → 7
SUMMER MATH WORKBOOK
Bridge Building Activities
Arithmetic
Algebra
Geometry and Statistics

Grade
8 → 9
SUMMER MATH WORKBOOK
Bridge Building Activities
Ratio and Percentage
Algebra
Geometry and Graphing

Grade
9 → 10
SUMMER MATH WORKBOOK
Bridge Building Activities
Factoring and Distributing
Algebra
Geometry and Graphing

Introduction

As parents and educators, we understand the pivotal role that mathematics plays in shaping a child's academic journey and future success. Yet, the path to mathematical proficiency can often seem daunting, filled with challenges and complexities. That's where the transformative power of Summer Bridge Building Activities books comes into play, illuminating the way forward with clarity, precision, and purpose.

Summer vacation is a time for rest and relaxation, but it also presents the risk of the "summer slide," where students lose some of the academic gains they made during the school year. Summer Bridge Building Activities books are specifically designed to tackle this challenge, ensuring that your child stays academically engaged and prepared for the upcoming school year. These books provide a seamless bridge from one grade to the next, reinforcing essential skills and introducing new concepts that will give your child a head start.

Imagine your child eagerly diving into the pages of a Summer Bridge Building Activities book, greeted by clear, engaging content that demystifies complex mathematical concepts. With each turn of the pages, they embark on a journey of discovery, encountering thoughtfully curated practice questions that reinforce learning and sharpen problem-solving skills. As they unveil the answers to those questions, a sense of accomplishment blossoms within them — a tangible reward for their hard work and dedication.

Summer Bridge Building Activities books transcend traditional educational tools; they are meticulously crafted to build a deep and enduring understanding of mathematics. These books follow a sequential and logical progression, starting from fundamental principles and advancing to sophisticated problem-solving strategies. Each chapter is designed to build on the previous one, ensuring a solid and comprehensive foundation for future learning.

Parents, we yearn for nothing more than to see our children thrive academically and personally. We want to witness the spark of inspiration ignited within them as they overcome academic challenges with confidence and poise. Summer Bridge Building Activities books serve as indispensable partners in this noble endeavor, offering not just practice questions but the keys to unlocking a world of academic and personal opportunities.

Visualize the pride on your child's face as they master a challenging math concept, the joy they experience when their efforts yield results, and the confidence they gain with each success. These pages are designed to make learning math a positive, enriching, and deeply rewarding experience that will benefit them throughout their academic journey and beyond.

For educators, Summer Bridge Building Activities books are invaluable allies in the quest to cultivate mathematical proficiency in the classroom. Accompanied by comprehensive guides and readily available answers, instructors can focus on mentoring and nurturing their students, secure in the knowledge that these books provide a robust framework for effective learning.

Within the pages of Summer Bridge Building Activities books lies not just the promise of academic excellence, but the seeds of a brighter future. By integrating these resources into your child's summer routine, you are bestowing upon them the gifts of confidence, curiosity, and a lifelong love of learning.

Invest in your child's future today with Summer Bridge Building Activities books — because every great journey begins with a single step, and this step can change everything. Keep the momentum of learning alive over the summer, and watch your child soar to new academic heights.

Contents

Grade
7 - 9
PRE ALGEBRA
WORKBOOK
BRIDGE BUILDING
ACTIVITIES
Equations, Inequalities
and Expressions
Linear Equations
Graphing and Slope
System of Equations
Quadratic Equations

Grade
6 - 8
PRE ALGEBRA
WORKBOOK
BRIDGE BUILDING
ACTIVITIES
Equations
One Side and Two Sides
Verbal Algebra
Expressions
Linear Equations and Slope
Order of Operations

Grade
5 - 6
PRE ALGEBRA
WORKBOOK
BRIDGE BUILDING
ACTIVITIES
Integers, Mixed Numbers
Decimals and Fractions
Place Value
Exponents and Roots
Percentage and Ratio
Word Problems

PRE ALGEBRA
WORKBOOK
for
Beginners
Integers
Fractions, Mixed Numbers
Place Value
Exponents and Roots
Percentage
Ratio Conversion

PRE ALGEBRA
WORKBOOK
for
Adults
Integers
Percent and Ratio
Equations, Inequalities
Expressions
Order of Operations

Grade
7 - 8
PRE ALGEBRA
WORKBOOK
BRIDGE BUILDING
ACTIVITIES
Equations, Inequalities
and Expressions
Verbal Algebra
Expressions
Percent and Ratio
Word Problems

Grade
9 - 10
PRE ALGEBRA
WORKBOOK
BRIDGE BUILDING
ACTIVITIES
Equations and Inequalities
Verbal Algebra
Linear and Quadratic
Equations
System of Equations
Polynomials

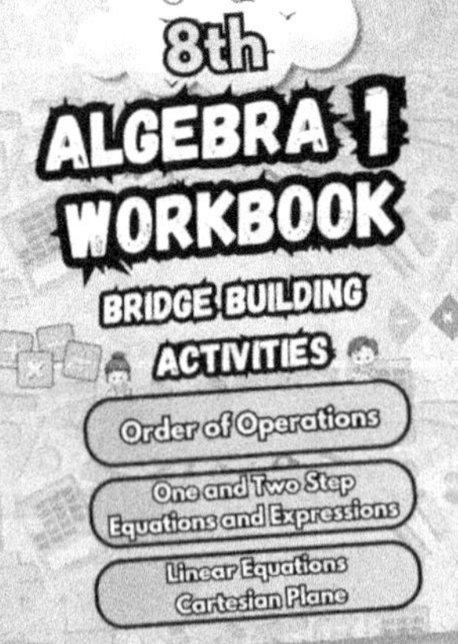
Grade
8th
ALGEBRA 1
WORKBOOK
BRIDGE BUILDING
ACTIVITIES
Order of Operations
One and Two Step
Equations and Expressions
Linear Equations
Cartesian Plane

Grade
7 - 9
ALGEBRA 1
WORKBOOK
BRIDGE BUILDING
ACTIVITIES
Integers
Order of Operations
One and Multi Step
Equations and Expressions
Linear, Quadratic Equations
Equations One Side, Two Sides

Operations with Integers

Positive and negative integers are whole numbers that can represent quantities greater than zero and less than zero, respectively.

Positive Integers: Positive integers are whole numbers greater than zero. They are denoted by the numbers 1,2,3,4...

Negative Integers: Negative integers are whole numbers less than zero. They are denoted by placing a negative sign ("-") before the numbers, such as $-1,-2,-3,-4,...$

The positive integers are used to represent the number of objects, scores, etc. whereas the negative integers can be used to represent debt, losses, temperatures below freezing points, etc.

Let's solve some problems:

1. $6 - (-8) - 9$

- Start by simplifying within the parentheses:

$$-(-8) \text{ becomes } 8.$$

- Rewrite the expression with the simplified part:

$$6 + 8 - 9.$$

- Now perform addition and subtraction from left to right:

$$6 + 8 = 1\,4, \text{ then } 14 - 9 = 5$$

2. $(-5) - (-3) + 10$

$$(-5) + 3 + 10$$

$$(-5) + 3 = -2, \text{ then } -2 + 10 = 8$$

Operations with Integers

1. $(-7) - (-4) =$

2. $2 + (-8) + 5 =$

3. $5 - 2 + 1 =$

4. $(-2) + (-7) =$

5. $6 - 3 + 7 =$

6. $4 + 10 - 4 =$

7. $(-3) - (-8) + 2 =$

8. $2 + 3 - 4 =$

9. $7 + (-4) + 9 =$

10. $(-7) - 8 + (-1) =$

11. $(-8) - (-7) =$

12. $(-5) - 9 + (-7) =$

13. $(-5) + (-9) =$

14. $(-9) + (-5) - 5 =$

15. $2 + 7 - 7 =$

16. $8 - (-7) =$

17. $7 - 10 + 3 =$

18. $(-9) - (-3) - (-9) =$

19. $(-4) + (-10) =$

20. $2 - 9 + 3 =$

21. $6 + (-4) - 8 =$

22. $(-9) - 10 =$

23. $(-8) - (-8) + 2 =$

24. $4 - 5 - 3 =$

25. $(-7) + (-7) =$

26. $(-3) - 6 + (-2) =$

27. $9 + (-8) =$

28. $7 + (-5) =$

29. $(-6) - (-6) + 7 =$

30. $(-1) - (-5) + 6 =$

31. $(-8) + 5 + (-3) =$

32. $5 + (-7) =$

33. $3 - 1 - 4 =$

34. $(-10) + (-5) + 2 =$

35. $(-7) + 6 + (-4) =$

36. $(-10) + 6 =$

37. $5 - (-2) - 4 =$

38. $3 - 7 - 7 =$

39. $5 - (-2) =$

40. $6 + 5 - 8 =$

41. $(-10) - 7 + (-7) =$

42. $(-5) - (-4) - (-10) =$

43. $3 - 10 + (-9) =$

44. $9 - 10 + (-7) =$

45. $(-3) - (-3) - (-1) =$

46. $(-10) + (-3) + 3 =$

47. $(-4) - 5 + (-10) =$

48. $1 + (-6) + 7 =$

49. $2 - (-9) =$

50. $(-1) - (-8) + 6 =$

51. $(-1) - 6 =$

52. $(-8) + 7 + (-6) =$

53. $10 + (-9) - 5 =$

54. $(-2) - (-2) + 4 =$

55. $(-8) - (-7) + 6 =$

56. $4 + 4 - 6 =$

57. $(-5) + 5 + (-8) =$

58. $7 - 3 + (-10) =$

Mixed Numbers: Mixed into Improper

Mixed numbers and improper fractions are two different ways to represent the same value of a fraction.

1. **Mixed Number:** A mixed number is a combination of a whole number and a proper fraction. For example, $2\frac{1}{3}$ is a mixed number, where 2 is the whole number part and $\frac{1}{3}$ is the fraction part.

2. **Improper Fraction:** An improper fraction is a fraction where the numerator is greater than or equal to the denominator. For example, $\frac{7}{3}$ is an improper fraction because 6 is greater than 3.

To convert a mixed number to an improper fraction, you multiply the whole number by the denominator of the fraction, add the numerator, and then write the result over the original denominator. For example:

$$2\frac{1}{3} = \frac{2 \times 3 + 1}{3} = \frac{7}{3}$$

To convert an improper fraction to a mixed number, we divide the numerator by the denominator. The quotient becomes the whole number part, and the remainder becomes the numerator of the fraction. For example:

$$\frac{7}{3} = 2\frac{1}{3}$$

<u>Mixed Numbers: Addition and Subtraction</u>

To add or subtract mixed numbers, we follow similar steps as when adding or subtracting regular fractions. For instance:

Addition:

- <u>Add the whole numbers:</u> Add the whole number parts of the mixed numbers together.
- <u>Add the fractions:</u> Add the fractions parts of the mixed numbers together.
- <u>Simplify (if needed):</u> If the fraction part of the sum is an improper fraction, simplify it by converting it to a mixed number.

Subtraction:

- <u>Subtract the whole numbers:</u> Subtract the whole number part of the second mixed number from the whole number part of the first mixed number.
- <u>Subtract the fractions:</u> Subtract the fraction part of the second mixed number from the fraction part of the first mixed number.
- <u>Simplify (if needed):</u> If the fraction part of the difference is a negative fraction, borrow from the whole number part or simplify it by converting it to a mixed number.

<u>**Mixed Numbers: Multiplication and Division**</u>

To multiply or divide mixed numbers, we follow these steps:

Multiplication:

- <u>Convert the mixed numbers to improper fractions:</u> Multiply the whole number by the denominator of the fraction, then add the numerator. Write the result over the original denominator.
- <u>Multiply the fractions:</u> Multiply the numerators together to get the new numerator and multiply the denominators together to get the new denominator.
- <u>Simplify (if needed):</u> If the result is an improper fraction, simplify it by converting it back to a mixed number.

Division:

- <u>Convert the mixed numbers to improper fractions:</u>
- <u>Invert the divisor:</u> Flip the second fraction (the one you're dividing by) so that the division becomes multiplication.
- <u>Multiply the fractions:</u> Multiply the numerators together to get the new numerator and multiply the denominators together to get the new denominator.
- <u>Simplify (if needed):</u> If the result is an improper fraction, simplify it by converting it back to a mixed number.

Mixed Numbers

Calculate.

1. $1\frac{1}{4} \div 5\frac{8}{9} =$ _______________

2. $5\frac{1}{2} \times 5\frac{1}{8} =$ _______________

3. $9\frac{7}{9} + 2\frac{1}{3} =$ _______________

4. $4\frac{2}{8} \times 6\frac{1}{2} =$ _______________

5. $5\frac{5}{7} \times 6\frac{7}{10} =$ _______________

6. $5\frac{2}{5} + 4\frac{1}{4} =$ _______________________

7. $7\frac{6}{7} - 7\frac{2}{4} =$ _______________________

8. $1\frac{1}{2} \div 7\frac{6}{10} =$ _______________________

9. $6\frac{4}{6} + 8\frac{3}{5} =$ _______________________

10. $5\frac{4}{8} \times 7\frac{2}{6} =$ _______________________

11. $4\frac{1}{5} + 2\frac{3}{4} =$ _______________

12. $9\frac{1}{8} + 6\frac{4}{9} =$ _______________

13. $3\frac{2}{3} \div 7\frac{1}{7} =$ _______________

14. $1\frac{1}{2} + 1\frac{3}{10} =$ _______________

15. $6\frac{4}{7} \times 3\frac{3}{8} =$ _______________

16. $8\frac{1}{4} \div 4\frac{2}{3} =$ _______________________

17. $9\frac{8}{9} - 6\frac{4}{5} =$ _______________________

18. $2\frac{1}{6} \div 1\frac{6}{10} =$ _______________________

19. $8\frac{1}{2} + 7\frac{9}{10} =$ _______________________

20. $1\frac{6}{7} \times 8\frac{1}{2} =$ _______________________

21. $7\frac{1}{3} \div 5\frac{3}{8} =$ _______________________

22. $1\frac{2}{4} + 5\frac{3}{6} =$ _______________________

23. $4\frac{1}{5} \div 4\frac{2}{9} =$ _______________________

24. $3\frac{4}{8} - 2\frac{4}{5} =$ _______________________

25. $8\frac{1}{4} \div 3\frac{1}{10} =$ _______________________

26. $6\frac{3}{9} \times 3\frac{2}{7} =$

27. $7\frac{1}{3} \times 1\frac{2}{6} =$

28. $6\frac{1}{2} \times 5\frac{7}{10} =$

29. $8\frac{1}{2} - 4\frac{1}{4} =$

30. $9\frac{7}{8} - 1\frac{1}{7} =$

31. $4\frac{4}{9} \div 5\frac{4}{6} =$ _______________

32. $9\frac{1}{3} + 8\frac{3}{5} =$ _______________

33. $3\frac{1}{5} + 5\frac{7}{9} =$ _______________

34. $9\frac{1}{8} - 7\frac{1}{3} =$ _______________

35. $4\frac{3}{4} - 3\frac{1}{6} =$ _______________

36. $9\frac{6}{7} - 4\frac{1}{2} =$

37. $4\frac{4}{10} + 7\frac{4}{8} =$

38. $3\frac{4}{5} + 9\frac{4}{9} =$

39. $9\frac{1}{3} \times 7\frac{8}{10} =$

40. $5\frac{3}{4} \times 3\frac{4}{7} =$

41. $4\frac{1}{6} \times 2\frac{1}{2} =$ ________________________

42. $4\frac{6}{9} \div 9\frac{4}{7} =$ ________________________

43. $2\frac{8}{10} \div 9\frac{1}{4} =$ ________________________

44. $8\frac{2}{6} + 7\frac{5}{8} =$ ________________________

45. $6\frac{3}{5} \div 6\frac{1}{3} =$ ________________________

<u>**Multiple Operations Fractions**</u>

Fraction multiple operations involve performing multiple arithmetic operations (addition, subtraction, multiplication, division) on fractions.

We follow (PEDMAS that stands for the order of operations in arithmetic) to solve multiple operations Fractions:

1. **Parentheses:** Perform operations inside parentheses first.

2. **Exponents:** Evaluate expressions with exponents or powers.

3. **Multiplication and Division:** Perform multiplication and division from left to right.

4. **Addition and Subtraction:** Perform addition and subtraction from left to right.

For example:

Let's solve the expression: $\frac{3}{4} + \frac{1}{2} \times \frac{2}{3}$

Step 1: Begin by performing the multiplication operation first:

$$= \frac{1 \times 2}{2 \times 4} = \frac{2}{6} = \frac{1}{3}$$

Step 2: Now rewrite the expression with the result of the multiplication:

$$\frac{3}{4} + \frac{1}{3}$$

Step 3: To add fractions, find a common denominator. In this case, the least common multiple (LCM) of 4 and 3 is 12.

Step 4: Rewrite both fractions with the common denominator:

$$\frac{9}{12} + \frac{4}{12}$$

Step 5: Add the numerators together and keep the common denominator:

$$\frac{13}{12} = 1\frac{1}{12}$$

Multiple Operations with Fractions

Find the solution.

1. $\dfrac{2}{9} + \dfrac{1}{2} - \dfrac{1}{2} =$

2. $\dfrac{3}{10} \times \dfrac{1}{6} + \dfrac{1}{2} =$

3. $\dfrac{1}{10} + \dfrac{7}{8} + \dfrac{1}{6} =$

4. $\dfrac{3}{8} \times \dfrac{3}{7} + \dfrac{7}{9} =$

5. $\dfrac{1}{4} \times \dfrac{1}{6} \times \dfrac{1}{2} =$

6. $\dfrac{2}{5} + \dfrac{1}{4} - \dfrac{1}{2} =$

7. $\left(\dfrac{2}{9} \times \dfrac{3}{8} \right) + \left(\dfrac{1}{8} \times \dfrac{2}{3} \right) =$

8. $\dfrac{1}{3} + \dfrac{3}{5} + \dfrac{3}{5} =$

9. $\dfrac{1}{4} + \dfrac{1}{6} + \dfrac{1}{10} =$

10. $\dfrac{3}{8} + \dfrac{1}{4} + \dfrac{1}{6} + \dfrac{3}{4} =$

11. $\dfrac{1}{2} + \dfrac{7}{10} - \dfrac{1}{2} =$

12. $\dfrac{2}{3} \times \dfrac{1}{4} \times \dfrac{1}{5} =$

13. $\left(\dfrac{2}{3} \times \dfrac{1}{2}\right) + \left(\dfrac{1}{10} \times \dfrac{1}{4}\right) =$

14. $\dfrac{2}{7} \times \dfrac{2}{3} + \dfrac{1}{5} =$

15. $\left(\dfrac{9}{10} + \dfrac{1}{2}\right) - \left(\dfrac{1}{5} \times \dfrac{1}{9}\right) =$

16. $\left(\dfrac{3}{10} + \dfrac{1}{3}\right) - \left(\dfrac{3}{8} \times \dfrac{1}{5}\right) =$

17. $\left(\dfrac{1}{6} + \dfrac{2}{3}\right) - \left(\dfrac{1}{10} \times \dfrac{5}{8}\right) =$

18. $\dfrac{3}{10} + \dfrac{1}{6} + 3 =$

19. $\dfrac{2}{7} + \dfrac{1}{10} + 6 =$

20. $\dfrac{2}{9} \times \dfrac{1}{10} + \dfrac{1}{4} =$

21. $\dfrac{2}{7} + \dfrac{1}{2} + \dfrac{1}{8} =$

22. $\dfrac{5}{6} + \dfrac{1}{7} + \dfrac{1}{2} + \dfrac{1}{6} =$

23. $\dfrac{1}{2} + \dfrac{3}{10} + \dfrac{2}{3} + \dfrac{1}{2} =$

24. $\left(\dfrac{5}{8} \times \dfrac{1}{4}\right) + \left(\dfrac{1}{2} \times \dfrac{1}{4}\right) =$

25. $\dfrac{3}{4} \times \dfrac{6}{7} + \dfrac{6}{7} =$

26. $\left(\dfrac{5}{8} + \dfrac{6}{7}\right) - \left(\dfrac{3}{4} \times \dfrac{1}{4}\right) =$

27. $\left(\dfrac{1}{7} \times \dfrac{3}{4}\right) + \left(\dfrac{1}{2} \times \dfrac{1}{2}\right) =$

28. $\left(\dfrac{1}{6} + \dfrac{2}{9}\right) \times \left(\dfrac{7}{8} + \dfrac{3}{4}\right) =$

29. $\dfrac{7}{9} \times \dfrac{1}{3} + \dfrac{4}{7} =$

30. $\dfrac{5}{9} \times \dfrac{1}{6} + \dfrac{1}{6} =$

Place Value and Expanded Notations

Place value tells us the value of a digit in a number based on where it's placed.

Imagine we have the number 2,735,987,647.52843. It has 15 digits.

Now, each digit holds a special place. Let's break down the number 2,735,987,647.52843:

- The digit 2 is in billions place. Its value is 2 × 1,000,000,000=2,000,000,000

- The digit 7 is in hundred millions place. Its value is 7 × 100,000,000=700,000,000

- The digit 3 is in the ten millions place. Its value is 3 × 1,000,000=30,000,000.

- The digit 5 is in the millions place. Its value is 5 × 1,000,000=5,000,000.

- The digit 9 is in the hundred thousands place. Its value is 9×100,000=900,000.

- The digit 8 is in the ten thousands place. Its value is 8×10,000=80,000.

- The digit 7 is in the thousands place. Its value is 7×1,000=7,000.

- The digit 6 is in the hundreds place. Its value is 6×100=600.

- The digit 4 is in the tens place. Its value is 4×10=40.

- The digit 7 is in the ones place. Its value is 7×1=7.

- The digit 5 is in the tenths place. Its value is $5 \times \frac{1}{10} = 0.5$.

- The digit 2 is in the hundredths place. Its value is $2 \times \frac{1}{100} = 0.02$.

- The digit 8 is in the thousandths place. Its value is $8 \times \frac{1}{1000} = 0.008$.

- The digit 4 is in the ten thousandths place. Its value is $4 \times \frac{1}{10,000} = 0.0004$.

- The digit 3 is in the hundred thousandths place. Its value is $3 \times \frac{1}{100,000} = 0.00003$.

When we add these values together, we find the value of the entire number:

$$2{,}000{,}000{,}000 + 700{,}000{,}000 + 30{,}000{,}000 + 5{,}000{,}000 + 900{,}000 + 80{,}000 + 7{,}000 + 600 + 40 + 7 + 0.5 + 0.02 + 0.008 + 0.0004 + 0.00003 = 2{,}735{,}987{,}647.52843$$

Place Value

Determine the place value of the underlined digit.

1. 17,352,460,375 = ___________________

2. 52,928,817.706 = ___________________

3. 82,982,001.58 = ___________________

4. 793,167,076.39 = ___________________

5. 9,641,986.4937 = ___________________

6. 6,861,078,275.2 = ___________________

7. 860,067.61586 = ___________________

8. 87,949,3_1_9,950 = _______________________

9. 1,945,639.45_9_8 = _______________________

10. 37,1_7_8,380.935 = _______________________

11. 30,439,071.3_6_2 = _______________________

12. 5,286,012.038_2_ = _______________________

13. 553,_6_59,372.33 = _______________________

14. 86,834,6_5_2.85 = _______________________

15. $6\underline{1},186,453,844$ = ___________________________

16. $40\underline{8},021.11574$ = ___________________________

17. $46,428,\underline{9}32,546$ = ___________________________

18. $\underline{5}8,881,869.138$ = ___________________________

19. $979,833.16\underline{7}77$ = ___________________________

20. $128,453,244.\underline{9}8$ = ___________________________

21. $12,8\underline{1}8,404,465$ = ___________________________

22. 301,2̲16,115.99 = _______________________________

23. 5,552,554.3̲045 = _______________________________

24. 55̲,575,896.867 = _______________________________

25. 177,2̲79.40887 = _______________________________

26. 8,642,284.9̲486 = _______________________________

27. 51̲,085,903,407 = _______________________________

28. 37,153,105.7̲67 = _______________________________

29. 81,855,297.35<u>4</u> = _______________________________

30. 387,628,301.<u>13</u> = _______________________________

31. 4,462,3<u>5</u>6.9298 = _______________________________

32. 9,202,615.427<u>3</u> = _______________________________

33. 32<u>7</u>,857.58619 = _______________________________

34. 2,522,<u>4</u>87.8953 = _______________________________

35. 196,9<u>5</u>9.60497 = _______________________________

36. 1,933,113.4_18_ = _______________________________

37. 6,0_34_,440,181.6 = _______________________________

38. 3_36_,080,443.17 = _______________________________

39. _2_45,786.08947 = _______________________________

40. _2_88,295,750.03 = _______________________________

41. 870,_5_47,472.94 = _______________________________

42. 3,_3_47,751,562.2 = _______________________________

Adding Decimals

Adding decimals is like adding whole numbers, but we must align the decimal points carefully. For instance, when adding 49.88 and 45.78:

Step 1: Align the decimal points.

$$49.88$$
$$+\ 45.78$$

Step 2: Start adding from the rightmost digit (the ones place) and move to the left.

Add 8 and 8: 8 + 8 = 16. Write down 6 in the ones place and carry over 1 to the tenths place.

$$49.88$$
$$+\ 45.78$$
$$6$$

Step 3: Add the tenths place.

Add 1 (carried over from the previous step), 8, and 7: 1 + 8 + 7 = 16. Write down 6 in the tenths place and carry over 1 to the hundredths place.

$$49.88$$
$$+\ 45.78$$
$$66$$

Step 4: Continue adding digits to the left until you reach the leftmost digit:

$$49.88$$
$$+\ 45.78$$
$$9566$$

Step 5: Finally, write the sum with the decimal point directly below the decimal points in the original numbers.

$$49.88$$
$$+\ 45.78$$
$$95.66$$

Subtracting Decimals

Subtracting decimals follows a process like adding decimals, except instead of adding the numbers, we subtract them.

Multiplying Decimals

Multiplying decimals is a lot like multiplying whole numbers, but we need to be careful about where we put the decimal point in the answer.

Step 1: Start by multiplying the numbers together, just like we do with whole numbers. Ignore the decimals for now.

Step 2: Count how many decimal places there are in the numbers we're multiplying. This will tell us how many decimal places our answer should have.

Step 3: Put the decimal point in the answer by starting from the right side of the number. Move the decimal point to the left as many places as there are in the total number of decimal places.

For example, let's multiply 4.5 by 2.5:

Step 1: Multiply the numbers as if they were whole numbers:

$$25 \times 45 = 1125.$$

Step 2: There is one decimal place in 2.5 and one in 4.5, making a total of two decimal places.

Step 3: Starting from the right side of the answer, count two places to the left and put the decimal point there.

So, the final answer is 11.25.

Remember to pay close attention to where the decimal point goes in the answer.

Dividing Decimals

Dividing decimals is a lot like dividing whole numbers, but we need to be careful about placement of decimal point in the answer.

Operations with Decimals

Complete the operations.

1.
$$\begin{array}{r} 9.5 \\ \times\ 7.6 \\ \hline \end{array}$$

2.
$$\begin{array}{r} 4.9 \\ \times\ 7.6 \\ \hline \end{array}$$

3.
$$3.9\overline{)6.3}$$

4.
$$\begin{array}{r} 2.2 \\ \times\ 5.2 \\ \hline \end{array}$$

5.
$$\begin{array}{r} 78.63 \\ +\ 78.28 \\ \hline \end{array}$$

6.
$$\begin{array}{r} 8.9 \\ \times\ 6.3 \\ \hline \end{array}$$

7.
$$\begin{array}{r} 13.48 \\ +\ 99.06 \\ \hline \end{array}$$

8.
$$\begin{array}{r} 82.80 \\ -\ 70.03 \\ \hline \end{array}$$

9.
$$\begin{array}{r} 75.84 \\ -\ 12.62 \\ \hline \end{array}$$

10.
$$\begin{array}{r} 62.40 \\ -\ 20.22 \\ \hline \end{array}$$

11.
$$\begin{array}{r} 8.2 \\ \times\ 2.2 \\ \hline \end{array}$$

12.
$$8.9\overline{)1.4}$$

13.
$$65.85 - 16.42$$

14.
$$4.8 \overline{)1.2}$$

15.
$$23.07 + 85.24$$

16.
$$4.4 \times 7.9$$

17.
$$7.2 \overline{)6.6}$$

18.
$$4.1 \times 3.0$$

19.
$$86.75 - 76.10$$

20.
$$39.06 - 16.17$$

21.
$$85.25 - 60.45$$

22.
$$6.8 \overline{)9.4}$$

23.
$$9.1 \times 5.3$$

24.
$$11.51 + 34.25$$

25. $98.16 + 59.21$

26. $61.61 - 55.83$

27. 7.6×7.2

28. 1.8×7.3

29. $7.0\overline{)7.9}$

30. $92.39 - 68.68$

31. $7.2\overline{)6.2}$

32. $69.33 + 84.24$

33. $40.98 + 77.70$

34. 6.4×3.3

35. $66.85 - 52.90$

36. $7.1\overline{)5.7}$

37.
$$2.9 \times 7.7$$

38.
$$2.6\overline{)1.9}$$

39.
$$95.14 + 89.79$$

40.
$$12.83 + 89.20$$

41.
$$64.80 + 24.44$$

42.
$$76.60 + 31.79$$

43.
$$8.6\overline{)3.4}$$

44.
$$64.82 - 46.91$$

45.
$$53.14 + 44.86$$

46.
$$89.96 - 29.35$$

47.
$$4.5\overline{)1.8}$$

48.
$$87.18 - 43.96$$

49. 47.65
$+ \ 13.84$

50. $3.0 \overline{)1.1}$

51. 18.98
$- \ 16.14$

52. $7.0 \overline{)1.5}$

53. $2.8 \overline{)5.9}$

54. $5.2 \overline{)9.3}$

55. 6.7
$\times \ 9.5$

56. 2.8
$\times \ 1.4$

57. 87.63
$- \ 67.16$

58. 63.46
$+ \ 23.43$

59. 68.39
$+ \ 92.73$

60. 40.77
$+ \ 70.32$

61. 70.89
     − 44.63

62. 5.5
     × 4.7

63. 2.0
     × 2.4

64. 51.47
     − 47.27

65. 7.5
     × 7.0

66. 97.48
     + 64.87

67. 8.9$\overline{)1.7}$

68. 7.0
     × 7.4

69. 5.9
     × 3.4

70. 7.6$\overline{)3.0}$

71. 51.35
     − 49.33

72. 49.62
     + 89.95

73.   15.53
        + 52.36

74.   38.58
        + 19.96

75. $9.0\overline{)6.8}$

76. $7.7\overline{)7.3}$

77.   6.5
        × 2.8

78.   32.04
        + 18.91

79. $7.9\overline{)9.3}$

80.   70.49
        − 43.25

81.   5.3
        × 8.6

82.   68.64
        − 59.43

83.   44.90
        − 27.42

84. $8.2\overline{)4.7}$

<u>**Exponents**</u>

An exponent tells us how many times a number (called the base) is multiplied by itself. It is written as a superscript to the right of the base number. For example, in 2^3, 2 is the base and 3 is the exponent.

Rules:

1. **Product Rule**: When multiplying powers with the same base, add the exponents.

$$a^m \times a^n = a^{m+n}$$

   For example:

$$2^3 = 2 \times 2 \times 2 = 8$$

$$3^2 \times 3^4 = 3^{2+4} = 3^6 = 3 \times 3 \times 3 \times 3 \times 3 \times 3 = 729$$

2. **Quotient Rule**: When dividing powers with the same base, subtract the exponents.

$$a^m \div a^n = a^{m-n}$$

   For example:

$$5^3 \div 5^2 = 5^{3-2} = 5^1 = 5$$

3. **Power of a Power Rule**: When raising a power to another power, multiply the exponents.

$$(a^m)^n = a^{mn}$$

   For example:

$$(2^2)^3 = 2^{2\times3} = 26 = 64$$

4. **Power of a Product Rule**: When raising a product to a power, distribute the power to each factor.

$$(ab)^n = a^n \times b^n$$

For example:

$$(2\times3)^2 = 2^2 \times 3^2 = 4 \times 9\ = 36$$

5. **Power of a Quotient Rule**: When raising a quotient to a power, distribute the power to the numerator and denominator separately.

$$\left(\frac{a}{b}\right)^n = \frac{a^n}{b^n}$$

For example:

$$\left(\frac{4}{2}\right)^3 = \frac{4^3}{2^3} = \frac{64}{8} = 8$$

6. **Zero Exponent Rule**: Any nonzero number raised to the power of zero equals 11.

$$a^0 = 1$$

For example:

$$7^0 = 1$$

7. **Negative Exponent Rule**: A negative exponent means the reciprocal of the base raised to the positive exponent.

$$a^{-n} = \frac{1}{a^n}$$

For example:

$$2^{-3} = \frac{1}{2^3} = \frac{1}{8}$$

To evaluate expressions with exponents, we can use:

- **Repeated Multiplication**: Perform the multiplication indicated by the exponent.

- **Using the Rules of Exponents**: Apply the appropriate rule to simplify expressions involving exponents.

Square Roots

The square root of a number is a value that, when multiplied by itself, gives the original number. It's denoted by the symbol $\sqrt{\ }$.

For example, the square root of 9 is 3 because 3 * 3 = 9.

Cube Roots

The cube root of a number is a value that, when multiplied by itself twice, gives the original number. It's denoted by the symbol $\sqrt[3]{\ }$.

For example, the cube root of 8 is 2 because 2 * 2 * 2 = 8.

Exponents

Convert the values.

1. $12^2 =$ _______________

2. $20^{-2} =$ _______________

3. $17^4 =$ _______________

4. $3^2 =$ _______________

5. $14^3 =$ _______________

6. $11^{-2} =$ _______________

7. $1^4 =$ _______________

8. $11^3 =$ _______________

9. $3^4 =$ _______________

10. $9^2 =$ _______________

11. $11^4 =$ ___________________

12. $17^{-3} =$ ___________________

13. $19^3 =$ ___________________

14. $17^3 =$ ___________________

15. $8^3 =$ ___________________

16. $5^{-2} =$ ___________________

17. $1^2 =$ ___________________

18. $12^{-3} =$ ___________________

19. $14^{-3} =$ ___________________

20. $1^{-2} =$ ___________________

21. $7^4 =$ ___________________

22. $5^2 =$ ___________________

23. $4^4 =$ ___________________

24. $10^{-3} =$ ___________________

25. $8^{-3} =$ ___________________

26. $15^4 =$ ___________________

27. $7^2 =$ ___________________

28. $7^3 =$ ___________________

29. $3^{-3} =$ ___________________

30. $2^{-2} =$ ___________________

31. $13^{-2} =$ ___________________

32. $13^4 =$ ___________________

33. $19^{-3} =$ ___________________

34. $10^3 =$ ___________________

35. $2^{-3} =$

36. $11^{2} =$

37. $18^{2} =$

38. $13^{-3} =$

39. $2^{3} =$

40. $20^{4} =$

41. $14^{-2} =$

42. $16^{-2} =$

43. $15^{-3} =$

44. $12^{3} =$

45. $13^{3} =$

46. $19^{4} =$

47. $4^3 =$ _______________

48. $3^{-2} =$ _______________

49. $6^2 =$ _______________

50. $5^3 =$ _______________

51. $9^{-2} =$ _______________

52. $16^3 =$ _______________

53. $20^3 =$ _______________

54. $17^{-2} =$ _______________

55. $4^{-2} =$ _______________

56. $16^2 =$ _______________

Square and Cube Roots

Calculate the root of each value.

1. $\sqrt[3]{125}$ = _______________

2. $\sqrt[3]{8}$ = _______________

3. $\sqrt[4]{81}$ = _______________

4. $\sqrt[3]{216}$ = _______________

5. $\sqrt{9}$ = _______________

6. $\sqrt{4}$ = _______________

7. $\sqrt[4]{625}$ = _______________

8. $\sqrt[3]{2,197}$ = _______________

9. $\sqrt[3]{6,859}$ = _______________

10. $\sqrt{441}$ = _______________

11. $\sqrt[4]{16}$ = _______________

12. $\sqrt{16}$ = _______________

13. $\sqrt[4]{1{,}296}$ = _______________

14. $\sqrt{8{,}836}$ = _______________

15. $\sqrt{100}$ = _______________

16. $\sqrt{2{,}025}$ = _______________

17. $\sqrt{64}$ = _______________

18. $\sqrt[3]{343}$ = _______________

19. $\sqrt{7{,}569}$ = _______________

20. $\sqrt[3]{4{,}096}$ = _______________

21. $\sqrt[3]{1{,}000}$ = _______________

22. $\sqrt[3]{1}$ = _______________

NAME: _______________

23. $\sqrt{625} =$ _______________

24. $\sqrt[3]{27} =$ _______________

25. $\sqrt{81} =$ _______________

26. $\sqrt[4]{4,096} =$ _______________

27. $\sqrt[4]{2,401} =$ _______________

28. $\sqrt{1} =$ _______________

29. $\sqrt[3]{729} =$ _______________

30. $\sqrt{6,889} =$ _______________

31. $\sqrt[3]{4,913} =$ _______________

32. $\sqrt[4]{1} =$ _______________

33. $\sqrt{841} =$ _______________

34. $\sqrt[4]{256} =$ _______________

35. $\sqrt{36} =$ _______________

36. $\sqrt[4]{10,000} =$ _______________

37. $\sqrt{576} =$ _______________

38. $\sqrt{3,136} =$ _______________

39. $\sqrt{49} =$ _______________

40. $\sqrt{144} =$ _______________

41. $\sqrt{7,396} =$ _______________

42. $\sqrt{5,929} =$ _______________

43. $\sqrt{900} =$ _______________

44. $\sqrt{25} =$ _______________

45. $\sqrt[3]{5,832} =$ _______________

46. $\sqrt[4]{6,561} =$ _______________

47. $\sqrt{7{,}225} =$ _______________

48. $\sqrt[3]{64} =$ _______________

49. $\sqrt{5{,}041} =$ _______________

50. $\sqrt{324} =$ _______________

51. $\sqrt{2{,}704} =$ _______________

52. $\sqrt{7{,}921} =$ _______________

53. $\sqrt{1{,}849} =$ _______________

54. $\sqrt{5{,}476} =$ _______________

55. $\sqrt{10{,}000} =$ _______________

56. $\sqrt[3]{512} =$ _______________

57. $\sqrt[3]{1{,}331} =$ _______________

58. $\sqrt{784} =$ _______________

59. $\sqrt{1,024} =$ _______________

60. $\sqrt[3]{2,744} =$ _______________

61. $\sqrt{289} =$ _______________

62. $\sqrt{3,249} =$ _______________

63. $\sqrt[3]{8,000} =$ _______________

64. $\sqrt{961} =$ _______________

65. $\sqrt{5,329} =$ _______________

66. $\sqrt{4,225} =$ _______________

67. $\sqrt{1,089} =$ _______________

68. $\sqrt[3]{10,648} =$ _______________

<u>**Percentage**</u>

Percentage is a way of expressing a number as a fraction of 100. It is commonly used to represent proportions, rates, and comparisons. The symbol "%" is used to denote percentages.

To calculate a percentage, we multiply the given number by the appropriate fraction or decimal equivalent.

How to calculate a percentage:

Convert Percentage to Decimal: If the percentage is given as a percentage value (e.g., 25%), convert it to its decimal equivalent by dividing by 100.

$$\text{For example, 25\% as a decimal is } \frac{25}{100} = 0.25$$

Multiply: Multiply the decimal equivalent of the percentage by the given number. This gives us the portion of the number that represents the percentage.

$$100 \times 0.25 = 25\%$$

Result: The result is the calculated percentage value.

For example, to calculate 25% of 80:

<u>Convert 25% to a decimal:</u> 25% = 0.25.

<u>Multiply 0.25 by 80:</u> $0.25 \times 80 = 20$. The result is 20.

Percentage

Find the percentage of given numbers.

1. ☐ of 200 = 120

2. ☐ of 100 = 20

3. 5% of ☐ = 15

4. 3% of 300 = ☐

5. 4% of ☐ = 36

6. ☐ of 300 = 900

7. 80% of ☐ = 720

8. ☐ of 300 = 45

9. 10% of ☐ = 60

10. 50% of 700 = ☐

11. 100% of ⬚ = 200

12. 30% of 200 = ⬚

13. ⬚ of 800 = 56

14. 75% of 90 = ⬚

15. 2% of 500 = ⬚

16. ⬚ of 900 = 9

17. ⬚ of 200 = 16

18. ⬚ of 40 = 28

19. 25% of 20 = ⬚

20. 9% of ⬚ = 72

21. 4% of 600 = ⬚

22. ⬚ of 600 = 120

23. ⬚ of 900 = 81

24. ⬚ of 600 = 18

25. ⬚ of 800 = 280

26. ⬚ of 600 = 150

27. 100% of 600 = ⬚

28. 8% of ⬚ = 56

29. ⬚ of 300 = 150

30. 7% of 300 = ⬚

Percent Word Problems

Percent word problems involve situations where percentages are used to calculate quantities or amounts. These problems often require converting percentages to decimals and then applying them to the given values.

For example:

Bella bought a pair of shoes for $90.00. If she paid an additional 90% for taxes, how much in total did she pay for the shoes?

- Bella bought a pair of shoes for $90.00.
- She paid an additional 90% for taxes.

Calculate 90% of $90:

Tax= 90% × 90

Tax= 0.90 × 90

Tax= $81

Add the tax amount to the original price:

Total cost= $90 + $81

Total cost= $171

Percent Word Problems

1. A person wants to make a 4% tip on a $75.00 meal. How much should the tip be?

2. A classroom has 90 students, of which 20% are girls. How many boys are in the classroom?

3. Adrian buys brushes for $75.00 to sell them in market. If he wants to earn 4% profit. What must be the selling price of brushes?

4. A teacher gave a math test with 75 questions. If a student got 68% questions correct, how many questions were correct?

5. A restaurant makes a pizza that is 50 inches in diameter. If they want to increase the size of the pizza by 2%, what will be the new diameter?

6. A school has 75 students. If 68% of them play football, how many students play football?

7. If the number 75 is decreased by 44%, what is the value of the new number?

8. A school has 75 students. If 44% of them play baseball, how many students play baseball?

9. A store has 100 folders. If 2% of them are sold at the end of the day, how many folders are sold?

10. Christian bought a bicycle that cost $5.00 when it was new. If he eventually sold it for 20% of the original cost, how much was it sold for?

11. Hailey bought a book for $75.00. If she paid an additional 4% for sales tax, how much in total did she pay for the book?

12. Raelynn bought apples for $75.00. If she paid an additional 4% for sales tax, how much in total did she pay for the apples?

13. A school has 15 students. If 20% of them play tennis, how many students play tennis?

14. In a survey of 5 people, 20% said they prefer cats over dogs. How many people prefer cats?

15. A store offers 2% discount on all products. If the sale price of flowers was 100, what was the original price?

16. A store offers 4% discount on all products. If the original price of cotton swabs was 75, what is the sales price?

17. In a class of 35 students, 20% are girls. How many are girls?

18. In a class of 50 students, 44% are boys. How many are boys?

19. In a class of 80 students, 5% of them are in the Math Club. How many students are in the Math Club?

20. A store offers a 2% discount on all items. If Aurora buys microphones originally priced at $50.00, how much money did she save?

Convert: Ratio, Fraction, Percent, and Decimals

1.

	Ratio	Fraction	Percent	Decimal
a.				1
b.		8/10		
c.	6:11			
d.				0.2
e.	2:13			
f.			33.3%	
g.		10/20		
h.		9/19		
i.			33.3%	
j.				0.833
k.		10/14		
l.				0.167
m.				0.312
n.			64.7%	
o.		14/17		

2.

	Ratio	Fraction	Percent	Decimal
a.			33.3%	
b.			50%	
c.			62.5%	
d.			83.3%	
e.	12:17			
f.				0.25
g.				0.429
h.	9:14			
i.	1:7			
j.			28.6%	
k.			65%	
l.		3/4		
m.	14:16			
n.				0.588
o.				0.875

3.

	Ratio	Fraction	Percent	Decimal
a.				0.455
b.				0.231
c.				0.143
d.				0.286
e.	7:9			
f.				0.6
g.		1/1		
h.			68.8%	
i.				0.25
j.			75%	
k.			66.7%	
l.				0.529
m.		11/20		
n.	1:15			
o.			12.5%	

ANSWERS

Page 1: Operations with Integers

1. -3	**2.** -1	**3.** 4	**4.** -9	**5.** 10	**6.** 10	**7.** 7	**8.** 1	**9.** 12
10. -16	**11.** -1	**12.** -21	**13.** -14	**14.** -19	**15.** 2	**16.** 15	**17.** 0	**18.** 3
19. -14	**20.** -4	**21.** -6	**22.** -19	**23.** 2	**24.** -4	**25.** -14	**26.** -11	**27.** 1
28. 2	**29.** 7	**30.** 10	**31.** -6	**32.** -2	**33.** -2	**34.** -13	**35.** -5	**36.** -4
37. 3	**38.** -11	**39.** 7	**40.** 3	**41.** -24	**42.** 9	**43.** -16	**44.** -8	**45.** 1
46. -10	**47.** -19	**48.** 2	**49.** 11	**50.** 13	**51.** -7	**52.** -7	**53.** -4	**54.** 4
55. 5	**56.** 2	**57.** -8	**58.** -6					

Page 7: Mixed Numbers

1. 45/212	**2.** 28 3/16	**3.** 12 1/9	**4.** 27 5/8	**5.** 38 2/7
6. 9 13/20	**7.** 5/14	**8.** 15/76	**9.** 15 4/15	**10.** 40 1/3
11. 6 19/20	**12.** 15 41/72	**13.** 77/150	**14.** 2 4/5	**15.** 22 5/28
16. 1 43/56	**17.** 3 4/45	**18.** 1 17/48	**19.** 16 2/5	**20.** 15 11/14
21. 1 47/129	**22.** 7	**23.** 189/190	**24.** 7/10	**25.** 2 41/62
26. 20 17/21	**27.** 9 7/9	**28.** 37 1/20	**29.** 4 1/4	**30.** 8 41/56
31. 40/51	**32.** 17 14/15	**33.** 8 44/45	**34.** 1 19/24	**35.** 1 7/12
36. 5 5/14	**37.** 11 9/10	**38.** 13 11/45	**39.** 72 4/5	**40.** 20 15/28
41. 10 5/12	**42.** 98/201	**43.** 56/185	**44.** 15 23/24	**45.** 1 4/95

Page 16: Multiple Operations with Fractions

1. 2/9	**2.** 11/20	**3.** 1 17/120	**4.** 473/504	**5.** 1/48

6. 3/20	**7.** 1/6	**8.** 1 8/15	**9.** 31/60	**10.** 1 13/24
11. 7/10	**12.** 1/30	**13.** 43/120	**14.** 41/105	**15.** 1 17/45
16. 67/120	**17.** 37/48	**18.** 3 7/15	**19.** 6 27/70	**20.** 49/180
21. 51/56	**22.** 1 9/14	**23.** 1 29/30	**24.** 9/32	**25.** 1 1/2
26. 1 33/112	**27.** 5/14	**28.** 91/144	**29.** 157/189	**30.** 7/27

Page 23: Place Value

1. 3 hundreds	**2.** 8 thousands	**3.** 0 tens
4. 9 ten millions	**5.** 7 ten thousandths	**6.** 2 tenths
7. 8 ten thousandths	**8.** 1 ten thousand	**9.** 9 thousandths
10. 7 ten thousands	**11.** 6 hundredths	**12.** 2 ten thousandths
13. 6 hundred thousands	**14.** 5 tens	**15.** 1 billion
16. 8 thousands	**17.** 9 hundred thousands	**18.** 5 ten millions
19. 7 thousandths	**20.** 9 tenths	**21.** 1 ten million
22. 2 hundred thousands	**23.** 3 tenths	**24.** 5 millions
25. 2 hundreds	**26.** 9 tenths	**27.** 1 billion
28. 7 tenths	**29.** 4 thousandths	**30.** 1 tenth
31. 5 tens	**32.** 3 ten thousandths	**33.** 7 thousands
34. 4 hundreds	**35.** 5 tens	**36.** 1 hundredth
37. 3 ten millions	**38.** 3 ten millions	**39.** 2 hundred thousands
40. 2 hundred millions	**41.** 5 hundred thousands	**42.** 3 hundred millions

Page 29: Operations with Decimals

| **1.** 72.20 | **2.** 37.24 | **3.** 1.6 | **4.** 11.44 | **5.** 156.91 | **6.** 56.07 |

7. 112.54   **8.** 12.77   **9.** 63.22   **10.** 42.18   **11.** 18.04   **12.** 0.2

13. 49.43   **14.** 0.3   **15.** 108.31   **16.** 34.76   **17.** 0.9   **18.** 12.30

19. 10.65   **20.** 22.89   **21.** 24.80   **22.** 1.4   **23.** 48.23   **24.** 45.76

25. 157.37   **26.** 5.78   **27.** 54.72   **28.** 13.14   **29.** 1.1   **30.** 23.71

31. 0.9   **32.** 153.57   **33.** 118.68   **34.** 21.12   **35.** 13.95   **36.** 0.8

37. 22.33   **38.** 0.7   **39.** 184.93   **40.** 102.03   **41.** 89.24   **42.** 108.39

43. 0.4   **44.** 17.91   **45.** 98.00   **46.** 60.61   **47.** 0.4   **48.** 43.22

49. 61.49   **50.** 0.4   **51.** 2.84   **52.** 0.2   **53.** 2.1   **54.** 1.8

55. 63.65   **56.** 3.92   **57.** 20.47   **58.** 86.89   **59.** 161.12   **60.** 111.09

61. 26.26   **62.** 25.85   **63.** 4.80   **64.** 4.20   **65.** 52.50   **66.** 162.35

67. 0.2   **68.** 51.80   **69.** 20.06   **70.** 0.4   **71.** 2.02   **72.** 139.57

73. 67.89   **74.** 58.54   **75.** 0.8   **76.** 0.9   **77.** 18.20   **78.** 50.95

79. 1.2   **80.** 27.24   **81.** 45.58   **82.** 9.21   **83.** 17.48   **84.** 0.6

Page 36: Exponents

1. 144   **2.** 1/400   **3.** 83,521   **4.** 9   **5.** 2,744

6. 1/121   **7.** 1   **8.** 1,331   **9.** 81   **10.** 81

11. 14,641   **12.** 1/4913   **13.** 6,859   **14.** 4,913   **15.** 512

16. 1/25   **17.** 1   **18.** 1/1728   **19.** 1/2744   **20.** 1

21. 2,401   **22.** 25   **23.** 256   **24.** 1/1000   **25.** 1/512

26. 50,625   **27.** 49   **28.** 343   **29.** 1/27   **30.** 1/4

31. 1/169   **32.** 28,561   **33.** 1/6859   **34.** 1,000   **35.** 1/8

36. 121   **37.** 324   **38.** 1/2197   **39.** 8   **40.** 160,000

41. 1/196   **42.** 1/256   **43.** 1/3375   **44.** 1,728   **45.** 2,197

46. 130,321   **47.** 64   **48.** 1/9   **49.** 36   **50.** 125

51. 1/81   **52.** 4,096   **53.** 8,000   **54.** 1/289   **55.** 1/16

56. 256

Page 41: Square and Cube Roots

1. 5   **2.** 2   **3.** 3   **4.** 6   **5.** 3   **6.** 2   **7.** 5   **8.** 13

9. 19   **10.** 21   **11.** 2   **12.** 4   **13.** 6   **14.** 94   **15.** 10   **16.** 45

17. 8   **18.** 7   **19.** 87   **20.** 16   **21.** 10   **22.** 1   **23.** 25   **24.** 3

25. 9   **26.** 8   **27.** 7   **28.** 1   **29.** 9   **30.** 83   **31.** 17   **32.** 1

33. 29   **34.** 4   **35.** 6   **36.** 10   **37.** 24   **38.** 56   **39.** 7   **40.** 12

41. 86   **42.** 77   **43.** 30   **44.** 5   **45.** 18   **46.** 9   **47.** 85   **48.** 4

49. 71   **50.** 18   **51.** 52   **52.** 89   **53.** 43   **54.** 74   **55.** 100   **56.** 8

57. 11   **58.** 28   **59.** 32   **60.** 14   **61.** 17   **62.** 57   **63.** 20   **64.** 31

65. 73   **66.** 65   **67.** 33   **68.** 22

Page 47: Percentage

1. 60%   **2.** 20%   **3.** 300   **4.** 9   **5.** 900   **6.** 300%   **7.** 900   **8.** 15%

9. 600   **10.** 350   **11.** 200   **12.** 60   **13.** 7%   **14.** 67.5   **15.** 10   **16.** 1%

17. 8%   **18.** 70%   **19.** 5   **20.** 800   **21.** 24   **22.** 20%   **23.** 9%   **24.** 3%

25. 35%   **26.** 25%   **27.** 600   **28.** 700   **29.** 50%   **30.** 21

Page 50: Percent Word Problems

1. $3.00   **2.** 72   **3.** $78.00   **4.** 51   **5.** 51   **6.** 51

7. 42   **8.** 33   **9.** 2   **10.** $1.00   **11.** $78.00   **12.** $78.00

13. 3   **14.** 1   **15.** 102   **16.** 72   **17.** 7   **18.** 22

19. 4   **20.** $1.00

Page 55:   Convert: Ratio, Fraction, Percent, and Decimals

1.

	Ratio	Fraction	Percent	Decimal
a.	1:1	1/1	100%	1
b.	8:10	8/10	80%	0.8
c.	6:11	6/11	54.5%	0.545
d.	2:10	2/10	20%	0.2
e.	2:13	2/13	15.4%	0.154
f.	1:3	1/3	33.3%	0.333
g.	10:20	10/20	50%	0.5
h.	9:19	9/19	47.4%	0.474
i.	3:9	3/9	33.3%	0.333
j.	5:6	5/6	83.3%	0.833
k.	10:14	10/14	71.4%	0.714
l.	1:6	1/6	16.7%	0.167
m.	5:16	5/16	31.2%	0.312
n.	11:17	11/17	64.7%	0.647
o.	14:17	14/17	82.4%	0.824

2.

	Ratio	Fraction	Percent	Decimal
a.	1:3	1/3	33.3%	0.333
b.	1:2	1/2	50%	0.5
c.	10:16	10/16	62.5%	0.625
d.	10:12	10/12	83.3%	0.833
e.	12:17	12/17	70.6%	0.706
f.	1:4	1/4	25%	0.25
g.	3:7	3/7	42.9%	0.429
h.	9:14	9/14	64.3%	0.643
i.	1:7	1/7	14.3%	0.143
j.	2:7	2/7	28.6%	0.286
k.	13:20	13/20	65%	0.65
l.	3:4	3/4	75%	0.75
m.	14:16	14/16	87.5%	0.875
n.	10:17	10/17	58.8%	0.588
o.	7:8	7/8	87.5%	0.875

3.

	Ratio	Fraction	Percent	Decimal
a.	5:11	5/11	45.5%	0.455
b.	3:13	3/13	23.1%	0.231
c.	1:7	1/7	14.3%	0.143
d.	4:14	4/14	28.6%	0.286
e.	7:9	7/9	77.8%	0.778
f.	3:5	3/5	60%	0.6
g.	1:1	1/1	100%	1
h.	11:16	11/16	68.8%	0.688
i.	2:8	2/8	25%	0.25
j.	15:20	15/20	75%	0.75
k.	4:6	4/6	66.7%	0.667
l.	9:17	9/17	52.9%	0.529
m.	11:20	11/20	55%	0.55
n.	1:15	1/15	6.7%	0.067
o.	1:8	1/8	12.5%	0.125